THE RAMAZAN LIBATION

OTHER BOOKS BY ALAMGIR HASHMI

The Oath and Amen (1976)
Pakistani Literature (1978)
An Old Chair (1979)
America Is a Punjabi Word (1979)
My Second in Kentucky (1981)
Commonwealth Literature (1983)
Ezra Pound (1983)
This Time in Lahore (1983)
Neither This Time / Nor That Place (1984)
The Worlds of Muslim Imagination (1986)
The Commonwealth, Comparative Literature
                        and the World (1988)
Inland and Other Poems (1988)
The Poems of Alamgir Hashmi (1992)
Sun and Moon and Other Poems (1992)

The Ramazan Libation

—— SELECTED POEMS ——

Alamgir Hashmi

with an introduction by
JOHN KINSELLA

ARC
PUBLICATIONS
2003

Published by Arc Publications
Nanholme Mill, Shaw Wood Road
Todmorden OL14 6DA, UK

Copyright © Aurangzeb Alamgir Hashmi 2003
Introduction copyright © John Kinsella 2003

Design by Tony Ward

ISBN 1 900072 10 6

Cover painting by Sardar Muahammad

The publishers acknowledge financial assistance
from the Arts Council of England, Yorkshire.

International Editor: John Kinsella

CONTENTS

from **MY SECOND IN KENTUCKY**

from **THIS TIME IN LAHORE**

from **NEITHER THIS TIME / NOR THAT PLACE**

from **INLAND AND OTHER POEMS**

from **SUN AND MOON AND OTHER POEMS**

INTRODUCTION

Of himself, the great Pakistani poet Alamgir Hashmi has written: "I was born in 1951 in Lahore, a city with distinctive flavours and ambience, where many diversions would have been possible. Somehow I began to take reading and writing for myself rather seriously from an early age. It was long before I could admit to anyone that I wrote in ways and forms which were not regarded by many around me as quite useful enough. Growing up in a home where several languages were spoken, often interchangeably, offered a multiple choice from which a definite answer was expected. Thus English has remained my first language, the only one in which I live while counting my blessings with the others." Hashmi, in this personal statement, goes on to talk about the cultural diversity of his education, and how every word he has written has entailed some kind of "private struggle". The issues of choice and the need to write poetry are intrinsically part of Hashmi's poetics, as much as the question of where a voice locates itself as it traverses cultures. Hashmi is a hybridiser of cultures on one level, but more than that, he is both participant and observer. His poetic persona is complex and multi-faceted, it can be at once ironic and deeply sincere, it can be Pakistani and American, it can be spiritual and materialist. Love in a Hashmi poem is never a series of emotional responses removed from their cultural implications.

Hashmi is a genuinely trans-cultural poet, with wide interests and diverse tastes. An internationalist, he travels widely. I first met Hashmi at the International PEN 62nd World Congress held in Fremantle, Western Australia, in 1995. Along with the poet Dennis Haskell, I edited a small selection of delegates' poetry entitled Sightings. The poem of Hashmi's that we included was 'Islamabad 1988', in which the co-ordinates of language and place are palimpsested, where different locations become infused in each other, in the fluidity of language, and where a place is also what it is because it's not another:

I am practising the saffron smile

these days; field days
if you look at my lovely sisters,

Vienna, Helsinki, Canberra.
I am really not so unnatural;

can see the point in having
a pair of fussy big brothers.

Even as I know that I am not
Phoenix – out of Arizona,

I have risen from the ashes,
and must fall in love again.

The personification of the city is not mere device here; it is at the core of the way Hashmi's voice both locates itself in its subject matter, and also retains distance. The poet is deeply implicated in the poem, yet also detached. One is left with the feeling that there is some kind of crisis of certainty, that belonging is an elusive factor in Hashmi's life and work.

A traveller, but more than that – a world citizen – living in places as diverse as Switzerland, the United States, and Pakistan, Hashmi's poems are full of shifts between places – slippages, the negotiation of geographic and cultural spatialities that I find so attractive as a multi-nationed reader. Critics call him a modernist, and taste and poetics often support this, but he's also a traditionalist. There's more than a post-modern touch to his use of traditional façades, with ironic twists and colloquial observations and disruptions that complicate any categorising. Book titles indicate the shifts: America Is a Punjabi Word (1979), My Second in Kentucky (1981), This Time in Lahore: New Poems (1983), and Neither This Time / Nor That Place (1984), among others.

A wonderful counterpointing of cultural co-ordinates, an irony that is never malicious but always savvy, a celebration and gentle chiding, can be found in the linguistically versatile 'America is a Punjabi Word'. This sequence is Hashmi at his most enthusiastic: a picaresque that becomes universalising:

21

We came down
via Detroit;
I fastened the seatbelts
fast.
I kept the eye-shutters
closed and told
my camel not to stop
even for a Coke,
until we were safely
down below the Ohio –
in the navel
of these states.

The play with orientalism and American pop culture is deft, and fair-humoured. Modernity as a Western construct is undercut by '24': "...We say, Let's go back / to the Old World / where people know what the / people and camels / are all about." – a questioning of and a challenge to the intellectual modernities he has absorbed as a traveller and scholar. 'Captain Kirk in Karachi' is a paradigm model of "hybridised" post-modernity – a brilliant de-colonial anti-epic, an explorer's accountability sheet: the New World colonising the Old over again, but an old world where people and camels are understood.

The poem 'Refugee Girl Makes Good' is scathing to the imperial cultures of refuge. This is Hashmi out of good humour, and in something approaching anger. The bitter irony of the refugee child who comes from terror gaining super-proficiency in English and acceptance by the Oxford establishment, speaks for "Those many who are not here". Hashmi wrote the poem after reading a report in Asiaweek, and this reportage is vital to the construction of something that Hashmi challenges:

Your teacher is proud and fond of metonymy.
He calls you a "shining example to us all."
And your own English is perfect
enough to say: "I love chips."

That metonymy links us by degrees of separation all back to the refugee being rescued in the South China Sea. We are all culpable – in her status as refugee, and her status as cultural convert. The so-called first world seems fragile and false, and yet the "third world" poet does not make himself immune from his own criticism. He is aware of linguistic and geographic self-ironies.

Hashmi tells tales in which he is implicated; in his poems the lyrical self avoids us. The "I" of 'Snow', a deeply personal pronoun (analogically, symbolically) – is offset by the voice of "ghastly white" snow, its confusion and mystery, the people who "talk like a Greek Chorus". It's the range of his voice and material, the willingness to travel wherever knowledge and experience might take him, that mark Hashmi as vital. He is also a political poet of courage, a poet of understanding, respect, and "justice". In a poem like 'Bahawalpurlog: In Seven Parts', he speaks from his own "zone", familiarity something gained by immersion, but never an immediate right. Hashmi never claims ownership or absolute authority – he respects difference too much for this.

Hashmi is also a translator, about which he says, "Besides English, poetry is being written in several languages in Pakistan – in Urdu, Punjabi, Sindhi, Pashto, Baluchi, Siraiki, Kashmiri, etc. I have translated some of it (originally written in those languages) into English, in the intervals between my own poems and critical writing, or upon request. English-language poetry in Pakistan is vibrant, and some of it has been described by critics as part of the best anywhere. It can be said to have a firm tradition and as more and more young people write, as I notice nearly every week, the stream will likely have a steady course. However it is seen in the world at large, English-language poetry represents some of the best modern poetry in the region." There is a generosity in this that is obvious, and it characterises Hashmi's interest in the community of poetry.

Though Hashmi has already been well published in Britain through his now out-of-print Oxford University Press A Choice of Hashmi's Verse, this is a new and vigorous selection that I hope shows the poet in all his diversity. His is a voice that belongs wherever it is read.

John Kinsella
York, Western Australia, August 2003

12

The Oath and Amen:
Love Poems (1976)

GHAZAL

Someone,
who has nothing to do with it, says,
you are leaving town
and this
is no longer
a secret between us.

With others around us
I needed courage
to greet you that day
when
that green hedge
proudly travelled between us.

All these days
I have thought to go round
or cross over
and whisper
why,
what is happening between us?

Why do they remind me
that you are leaving?
And why don't I simply
stop
or talk to you
before this happens between us?

But,
if you must go away,
must I climb
that high, jealous growth
to settle
the things between us.

America is a Punjabi Word (1979)

AMERICA IS A PUNJABI WORD

Beginning where They Began

means I can talk
to the Governess of this
poem without taking
off her clothes.

                    Granted
Punjabi is not the tongue
for truth whose subject
is dubious: everything
it says turns mepoorgirl's
phrase frighteningly.

What is it I utter in this
dream of language,
the world nothing but
an alphabet,
myself the letter
that fell off the page?
A camel could as easily
be it. Take a cow,
if you like.

Words like log-cabins
are full of hay.
Resonance leaves them.
Light leaves them.
Leaves them.
Meaning was a posh
colony anyway. Now the
houses are in disrepair.
We leave them.
Our breath is a coin
we cannot pay.

We ask Space to take
us on his extended arm,
habitual as a coat.
We are men in passage.
Women take us as the earth
its squatters. It is
Journey, a road condition
with high tolls,
the traveller a huffing,
adamant fool who thinks
he will squeeze distance
out of God's galaxies

like orange-juice,
and then sell time cheap
to an old junk shop.
A sprinkle of sunlight,
and to him the earth looks

orange.
Like an orange?
I do not protest,
I do not sing,
I do not say anything.
I merely speak, and as I
slang my tongue into vacancy,
Old Girl – who made
the fragile things arrive
and grow safely,
you behave.

1

I was in New York.

I went up an
updated pyramid.

2

Might I be helped?
Could I rent a room here?

At the counter she sat,
a proper name
like a polished table:
"What do you mean?"

Dear lady,
do not ask me;
I am not your hieroglyph.

3

I was written in,
finally, and given
room.

              The ceiling
was the sky,
its million
wall-paper stars
to presage action.

4

I looked at the mirror
on the dressing-table:
a cloud was writing
out itself,
as I smoked.

It became a camel
freed from
a U-Haul cart
in Karachi;
its hump
the difficult curve
of the earth.

5

Boarded this desert-ship.
How good to board it
held up to space
like a present.

While there's nothing
to munch on sand,
it had a continent to graze
it hobbled on.

America was one leap
of the lunar year,
whose every
thirtieth day is suspect.
But no particular moon
shone here.

It hobbled on, and grazed.
I was asleep
before I could see
the cud.

6

Banished into sleep,
I was sent out

of the city.
Names crowded
along the zigzag
trail;
spectators
whose eyes like
welcome-sings
soon become
speed-barriers:
Maryland, Virginia
for Lovers, Norfolk
unto the Navy, and
North Carolina
where all the
dogwoods grow.

7

Other times, rain
washed over the leaves.
I went out walking,

picking out stars
from the street-puddles
of night.

Thus,
though I lost the minute,
I kept the time.

8

Etcetera
on the Sunset Beach
where I sandwiched
my couple of days
with peanut butter
and jelly.

In Myrtle Beach,
close by, though
further south,

James Dickey,
author of "The Lifeguard",
swam the
perilous sea
and saved the lost souls,
while his poetic-page,
the lifeguard,
failed to pick the
bodies. Dickey married

one from there. The
lifeguard has probably
gone to hell.
There I did not go.

9

A year went by.
I was lame in the
dogwoods.
Another summer and
spring went by.
It was a stop-over,
not a place to stay,
though the leaves
fell to the ground
like a rainbow.
I bought my camel
some new seatbelts
and said go.

Washington, D. C.

The Bicentennial
was all happening there.
A camel-dance followed.
All the girls
loved it; menfolk jeered.
We came out even,
tip-toe.

10

It was a swift summer.

I rolled my tongue
round the ice-lolly

in purple shade
drip

before the leaves
came down again.

11

I refuse to take the
Wall Street to a China
orange.

Moreover, my camel
resents
proverbiality.

As I must give him
grist not abominable
porridge,

I forsake this
line of argument,
omit

the wheeling about
in Wheeling,
West Virginia

and all the surrounding
coal-mines
whose miners are

too deep in the ground
to know. We are
in Kentucky.

12

The first in Kentucky
was a buck-shot.

My second is in
      other time,

another place.

13

Here I am tying
my camel to a tree.

This is Louisville
in Kentucky.

14

As I work on
straightening

the South's
dogtail accent

by displaying
the cylindrical

goodies from
England,

my camel sniffs
at the women's

dolman sleeves
and snorts all day.

15

As I ride one day
by a Gulf station,

ignoring a long queue
of embarrassments,

I pat my camel
on the neck,

while he whistles a
long whistle and moves

apace in a crisis
of good nerves.

America, you aren't short.
Your love is on reserve.

16

I briefed my camel
on good behaviour.
He was mouthing
election peanuts.
No one knew which way
the wind blew,
or which side
the camel would sit.

I pulled the reins.

Corpus Christi sat
by the Gulf of Mexico
dipping its heels
in the water.

17

The Grand Canyon
we easily climbed
across — not to
linger in acidic
images of barrenness.
That
river is haunted,
not sacred;
no Abyssinian lass
sings anything.

Albuquerque was too
hot; my camel prefers
north.

California Okies,
we rode along
the flower-decked
coast.   The Pacific
under, the hills
on the side,   the sky
just above us,
geography being
the completest thing.

18

From Redwoods
and the heavenly forests
that cover your north,
we emerged – the nomads –
in Vancouver,
glimpsing Chief Seattle's
timber town.

Ports are too olfactory,
offering fast dreams
of long voyages and
fresh salmon.
We avoided the more exotic
smells of the Indian Bazar.
A few apricots,
and we turned east,
spitting stones.

19

The long road
to the Niagara Falls
led us kindly.
In the flatlands
the grain-elevators
craned their necks
to utter greetings
of the wheatfields.

20

The Niagara district
switched off the cheer.
A river fell
in a
chasm.
It broke its knees
and wept.
A steam of tears arose
from below.
Japanese cameras
clicked all round.
I wonder if any
lens can take that
picture.

21

We came down
via Detroit;
I fastened the seatbelts
fast.
I kept the eye-shutters
closed and told
my camel not to stop
even for a Coke,
until we were safely
down below the Ohio –
in the navel
of these states.

22

This inset happened
elsewhere,
but better put in
than left out
altogether.

I met a female
of my own species
in the dogwoods
long ago. She was
with me, too,
though unaware
of our quadruped
companion.

23

In a close encounter
of the fourth kind,
I let her in on us.
My camel is indifferent.
She feels wiretapped,
cheated.

24

Anyway, the three of us
are now back in Louisville.
The time we were here last
has elapsed since. Neighbours
have retrieved their amazed
look. We say, Let's go back
to the Old World
where people know what the
people and camels
are all about.

25

We pack, we leave,
we go – hobbling
and grazing.

It is the sands send up
palms
becoming documentary.
Our zest

is a parachute blown full.
It comes from an orange,
I say. She disagrees
with a lemon-peel.
We choose a neutral country
as the place to land,
a grassy plot in the hills.

She and I are recognised
and given permission.
But the borderguard

denies visa for my
ruminating friend.
His tail is too short,
he says: this hobbledehoy
will not pass the customs.

26

We send him back.
He is not sad:
it's better to roam
about in New York
than go to a land
where they can't tell
a camel from the cows

that they have got.

27

Missing my camel,
I go to the Punjab.
This is no
thoughtless desert;
new beliefs
unfurl seasonally
as banana leaves,
people going bananas.
No camel is like him.
He is an absence
they do not know.

They still use his clan
to convey
the watermelon of doubt
from house to house.

28

The Swiss are still recusant.
They will not let him
enter their zone of neutrality,
as they didn't Jimmy Joyce
at first. They say, But Joyce
was so much better than this camel.

29

Happy New Yorkers,
if on a bright golden day
in Manhattan or Broadway
you run into a creature
you haven't known
or know only slightly
as you might the fog in Labrador,
an animal thinking, jestful,
big, long and gentle, whose spirit
is not down even on Mondays,
companionable as the Normandy air,
don't be afraid. Go forward
and give him a nosegay of marigolds,
and you will know what to make
of a camel.

30

The mayor
beams down the street,
reading a new sign:

SPEED LIMIT
5MPH
CAMEL CROSSING

Camel Crossing?

My Second in Kentucky (1981)

HARVEST HOMECOMING

Place, New Albany.
Time, above the Ohio.

The harvest homecoming
is over; the festival
is unhinged from the ground,
one plank unnailed from
another. The town
tired and vibrating
with chocolate giggle
goes walking home; hot dogs
and cotton candies all at
peace with each other,
weather somewhat too clear
to comment
carelessly.

Thirst is one thing
clearly absent. In Lahore
I have walked every street
with a burning Sahara
on the tip of my tongue.
Year upon year, I have walked
the streets here also, talking
to statues when men were dull
and women too busy, reading
wall posters in lamp light,
and seen time trickle down
like a sun-hit icicle.

I try to catch the cool air
with my hands, and failing,
leave the space to its grey
and green harmony

where the land and plants
inhabit each other.
And the farmers do not kiss
the holy stones.

The park is empty. The swallows
that announce the spring
are still far from here. And
the ababeels of Mecca
no more carry stones
in their beaks.

The believing soul croons
on the possible bush, and the
vintage banyan root is not
its home; its song is made
of the cricket and grass
celebrating a conspiracy
of colour.

When the sickles are laid
to rest in Lahore, or here,
the machines are stowed away,
the sun comes punctually along,
each insect ordered to its best
behaviour. Every ear of the corn
listens to its conscience,
supplications for a tidy crop
left to the mongrels.

Turned off the lamp
and pretended to myself
that I would be asleep
soon. Minutes later,
I heard a car crash into
a tree. I knew it;
the sound bears testimony
to its own danger.
Wore my slippers and gown
and went out. The night
was filled with blue lights
of emergency. When I went
back in, a dream from last
night twirled in front
of me: a cuckoo shook its
feathers in the attic
and flew off on one wing.
Each feather was a different
shade of night, weaving
a black knitout of time.

Near-morning, handling
the canny texture of words
I wished myself the brittle
silence of an egg-shell –
to shut up and sleep off
the whole year.

Tibet reads in Urdu
like tit:
pebbles and palindromes

are soft in the hills
below the world's
plateau. Elsewhere,

for instance Karachi,
that sits on the sea
like a paper-weight,

sand finds the
sandways,
a sola hat hooded on

a tropical phrase.
The clock strikes noon
cork-dry; to the sun's

logic, heat alone
is the answer.
The radio palms bear

the news of the north,
where Marco Polo sheep
are grazing away

the tops of our mountains.
And an occasional rain
washes the news away.

WE ARE BAFFLED BY DEATHS

We are baffled by deaths
on way to the barber shop.
A haircut seems
so unimportant.

When they raise the cot
to shoulders
and the procession forms
its dignity,

a bar of soap or chocolate
looks so out of place,
so mean.
Some old men

comb their beards
between the fingers,
and the young stand aside

to give way to those
who pass
or pass away.
Men on counter

stay away from money
as if something
had happened.
So some customers.

Only self-minding children
know the time to desist,
from amazement once again
break into play.

'As the snow-bound trade of the North comes down
To the market square of Peshawur town',
I quote from Kipling
and tell them how

the dwellers of the harsh
Northwest, the Pathans –
in English idiom pre-'47 –
had to rhyme with 'batons'.

The Southern Plains were better used –
stupefied in 110-degree heat,
when wild flower began to fleck
the tops of the Hindu Kush;

it was spring.

Once you are here, you find
stunning extremes prevail:
old ambuscades echo in the space
gnarled like mountains.
(You are hearing yourself!)
This sound is no match for the placid,
unmusical water from a scullery-maid's pail.
The unruly Swat River,
for instance, tosses out history
like a squirming catch
which must sell. We are buying
two thousand years, in the marketplace
down in Peshawar,
by a spit-and-polish street lamp
snuffed hours ago.
And it's been fifty years at least

that the ruble lost its shine
in these parts: no caravans of silk,
furs, and goldthread from Samarkand and
Bukhara now;
our cloth, indigo, tea, and mascara
we keep for ourselves.
From the silk we have or can borrow,
a ribbon now ties 'Pindi to Kashgar;

and time seems tied in the same knot.
I wonder what is lost.
This is still Peshawar, sister to Civilisation.
A place of winding alleys,
noise and intense aromas,
dense with shops, cyclists, horse-drawn
tongas, carts pulled by water-buffaloes
and put-putting

three-wheel taxis. Few street signs,
yet this baffling warren knows
a logic of arrangement. Out in Dera,
shotguns sell disguised as canes
and a ballpoint pen can kill!
Here, at one end of Qissa Khawani,
the Street of the Storytellers,
you can seek out

Misgaran Bazar for copper and brass goods.
Or you can turn in to Namakmandi,
the salt market,
also home to the false-teeth makers;
you can't miss
their grinning signs. And, who knows? you are

looking for grass prayer-mats of Pathan Bazar
or pitchforks made of bent sticks,

and charpoies –
both the bed and settee of the country.
One of us asks the price as the others prepare
to walk to the poppy fields out there.
I sit on one to test
and suddenly hear a shot at close distance.
No one in haste. I hope no one
tried to write home with a ballpoint pen.

Against the orange sky
our cornice-crows lift
their wings.
The grass can sleep.

Steadfast faith scuds
to the mosque on two legs;
piety belches
a fast or two
and prayers whirl like ghosts
in urban wind.

Your awry visions may fly up
but no stars will break.
(Hush Devil).
The grass can sleep.

SITTING IN

1

When seasons change,
they do not shake hands;
it just happens.
The buttoned sprig in the vase
rises, looks a branch; looks
greener or more grey,
brighter or dim.
The light cannot tell.

At night, I look at my city.
The dew settles on the leaf,
steeples salivate in the fists.
I still myself.
But the willows in the yard do not
listen. They rustle softly by.
So the morning is known to windows
by its smoke. The sun goes up,
then plunges on the roofs.

2

Give me your hand.
See, the forehead melts like glass.
In a moment, cold.
So when the light falls
on the enamelled dogtooth
of a prayer,
the mosque and the steeple
needle the shadow of God distantly.
Then, suddenly, the dead pan dish
hands are thrown in his face.

Mornings are a different matter.
The frocks open or close
like umbrellas.
The spirits of the sun
giggle in the bottles like mermaids.
The windows are blown
eastly shining as bubbles.
We close them.

The Ravi bounced,
water was measuring against tall men.

In another hour, it climbed the housetops.
Then,
all were crying

snakes were riding the wave. Handed
the secret on the left bank,
we were thrilled

and, slightly, anxious. Men were coming,
buffaloes and women lashed on
by water. Here were seven

corpses examined: they did not have
proper circumcision and, worth-drowning,
were sent washing

ahead. A man with spare pajamas was
suspect: 'There, a squatter!'
A straw could sting.

Sunday,
all left-bankers gathered on the bridge
to see the snake jungle

and each finger spotted a different thing.
Since all was coming down
from a land once

owned by us, some thought maybe
Agra would now come floating
with its marble minarets. And there were

those who stood unperturbed like the date-tree
and took the clearance.

What a bragbreath was
it my luck to have.
Three bigghas of land, and he
brags there's none like him
in day or nightrack.

How he cadged around for seven years
before the flood and after.
He was never more than a beggar.
Alas. My father, always-white-collar,
apple-cheek,
the known merchant of Gujrat.

Every morning I feel
I slept with a cactus.
Bragbreath.
What tree-branches they use
here to brush their teeth.

Back home, all Gujrat was after me.
I wonder how those boys
– so able, so gentle –
survived my marriage
after swearing so much.
One is a Magistrate; the other
Senator; and another
I have never known exactly what.
Times change.

Now the fields are pearled with rice
and fattening with potatoes.
Pearl-edged, he surely coddles
the young milkmaids,
soiling their jasmine days.
The farm-bed stays green
even as it rains

or the bush-burning sorrow
is at hand.

Alas my father. His loyalty even took
him for a relative.
Look at his shirt on the door.
Dirt, and so much of it.
There is no button on the collar.
Oh, where is my needle,
where is my thread?
Only a sodden ring
my father gave for marriage.

My pitchered zinnias are black in the sun.
And the flowers I chose for the evening
are rapt in the evening,
mistless,
like faces freckled in the
village winter.

What comes with the years, they say,
abides;
hardly known,
but understood.
It saves the questions
and paisas in its coin pockets,
and keeps the exits open.

Winter fires burning;
hens by the cockshut;
charpoies.

They waited by the hour.
These country bumpkins
toss in the spring.

How Gautum had succumbed
to the spirit;
a seduction that made him
desert the shadiest groves
of love and irrigated rice-
fields;

or how he had widowed his wife
in his life is painfully
familiar. Then let's celebrate
the discontent that fell upon him,
the unhappiness of a fine brain
that seeks employment,

the leisure which brims over a
summer holiday and must return
to the dull sanity
of routine.
He broke the pattern:
there could have been wrong

analogies; a Thoreau by the pond
sunk in meditation
to flee his taxes,
unperturbed by the vagrant callers.
He was glad that no pond
reflects much in the winter.

As always, the summer had a kind
of persistence in the
last. At night
Gautum went to his wife's room
and saw her sleep lit by an oil-lamp,
the infant sleeping sweetly

surrounded by the flowers.
He wanted to bow to kiss them.
But the fear prevented him, lest
he should awake his wife. Or was it
the old rule that one should
let a sleeping girl lie?

No one knows; but only
that he softly dropped his clothes
on the threshold – happy aimlessness –,
        mounted his horse
in the bright Indian moonlight,
        and rode off.

1

It is the coming of autumn, not the time to sing.
After days the sun looks out of the cloud.

The leaves in the corners of streets,
loose on the ground, curt beneath the feet, are dead.

Last summer the monsoon painted our sighs green
and the faces looked like fourth-grade watercolour.

Or was it the bush that has emptied its birds
and can have rain only, for it is the coming of autumn?

2

The flame in the lamp mumbled. In the morning,
I saw blessings hung in the leaves of a mango tree and the koel
sing.

Deep in the statistical pit of my heart grows the guava,
for the rose-garden is a dead issue.

Another day. A return to the less blue air
and dusty bread of fulfilment, in stone, whither?

3

Perhaps if you look long enough, for an intent eye
there may be a piece of a star wandering in the sky.

Eyes are the graves to bury stars and sleep
for it is the coming of autumn, not the time to sing.

The climate of this zone is writ in italic.
And mind overrules the littoral regions of country.

Drought tells its dry tales upon tongues that crackle
grudging the distant colours of the rainbow,

lacking as we do the ancient tyranny and rain-laden winds
that descend from the northern mountains.

4

Apples are ready to be picked, and frost dulls
the purple brinjal. I am reading the paper. I am still wonder-
ing.

In all art galleries of Lahore I have seen
portraits of peaceful citizens. Not one is worthy, not one.

I have stood long enough under the almond tree
to see sleep twinkle in my eyes, as if in a mirror.

In this air no bird flies to the orchard, only rumours.
There is always something in man's way. It is the air this time.

I think I'll go now and take new pictures.
This place is too old for me. This sun is too old for me.

This Time in Lahore (1983)

This time in
Lahore was upside down.

My flight was smooth,
a taxi drove me home.
My father had not yet
finished shaving –
but he didn't care
this morning. Mother
said she was listening
for a knock at the door,
but will I leave again?

She had put on age
around her temples
where father seemed
to have used a dye.

Answers could wait.
Brothers and sister came
and we sat round one another
long in the June heat
cooling in the shade
of time together.

I checked my books,
still wet from the last
monsoon; they looked whole
until you opened one.
Worms had chewed the print
and made studious
tunnels from cover to cover.

So was I feasted
everywhere I went,
at the friends' and relations',
who were most kind
and curious:
why in the world did I stay
so far away?
Everyone said I should
come back home.
Come back! Come back!
Come back!
It was hard to say.

I asked my old girl out.
She gave me a four-year long
look and put on her sun-glasses.
Where did I mean to take her?
Wicked movies off the reel,
in the Ramazan?
But we could perhaps
take a walk
and stop for a kulfi in
Jinnah Gardens?

Two days later
I saw a new sign by
the gate, the posted hours
of the military command
and procedures for those
who seek an audience.
A soldier at the garden gate
told me off to park a jeep.

I told mother
I will not stay very long,
and I do not hope to turn again.
I remember the story she told
me as a child: ...
the prince in his quest
goes over a bridge
in the valley of voices;
he hears his name called
from every foot-slab of distance
behind him, but he must not
turn back to listen.
If he does, he will turn
            to stone.
If he does not,
he can keep on going.

I have since seen statues
of heroes in the public gardens.

No prince,
but my quest will stay
as it began.
I am passing over the bridge
now, holding that blue dream over me
like a canopy of some such beneficence,
and pretending to be deaf,
sometimes even mute.
Dear mother,
send the morning-star my way.

SNOW

The blizzard overnight.
We wake up
to crazy things:

the pine trees rinsed in ice,
their glass twigs shattered below.
Our brains like eggs scrambled,
after dim sleep and snow.

What can one make of snow
this late,
ice-filled
chrysanthemums
pinned to the window?

No thought in winter would
burn
itself to fragrance,
or summer wit.

In this ghastly white,
when I want to say I am afraid
and wordless,
I cannot breathe my breath.

I have seen it happen.
Once stealthily
as in the grey, white, off-white
hair in my father's beard
which the razor has never let
anyone see.

            And the day
dazzled by the light of his commitment
he frowned –
it is not right
to be on the wrong side
of things –
he was already losing weight.
            And two years later
two more wrinkles on the face
made him forever angry.

Here people talk like a Greek chorus.

As I eat in my thoughts
at breakfast
like the latent haze ahead,
I feel this morning's
three-inch ice
    lapse underfoot,
and my eyes spill
with the salt sheet of snow.

THE BOAT PEOPLE

1

Plymouth is no longer
among safe destinations.
The rock is political;
it says: one Mayflower
isn't two in June.
Queen Isabella and Ho Chi Minh
need send no envoys; it's late.

Left to the wind and the sails,
they say, the vessels begin
to assert their will;
they will not go that way.
But Terra Incognita
and the inhospitable seas
in between?

Some have not given up.
The war and famine and other
well-wishers have torn them
to shreds even the wind
will not take: these boat people,
who have no papers to show,
where should they go?

2

Sometimes a boat
thinks she has made it.
Here's one which has escaped

the ASEAN, the U. S. Marines,
even the U. N., the Red Cross and the Crescent,
and the sea itself.

Docked in Darwin,
it awaits verdict:

'What you don't even have
your birth certificates,
or domicile?'

'You mean you kept no copies?'

'But you don't really fit
the going definition of a refugee.'

A greengrocer from Pursat
pleads in a waterlogged accent.
A schoolmaster from Vung Tau
claims he knew Captain James Cook,
personally, and recites Latin names
from a rumpled map.

The translator is on hand;
he's an expert on fiction –
'This story does not hold up.'

And then a sympathetic policeman –
'Sorry folks,
you've missed your boat.'

Whatever the fall in centimetres,
the desert knows a raincloud
from its look:
someone's emissary,
bearer of goodwill for those thirsting
            (for miles the veils fall,
the curtains ring);
but like a rich relative,
polite, squinting, glad to leave.

This summer has been hopeless
till this week.
The King's holiday in schools
to pray for rain
may be an adviser's mischief,
but the Namaz-i-Istisqa,
this Arabic petition on the earth's behalf,
may make even Nature
acquire a heart.

Some lands fear the sinful wet,
spoiling sport,
the inviting outdoors of lush weekends;
they cannot commit themselves
to a private silence
(as of the desert sands),
the sex in things interior.

A loud babble rises from the prayer-mats:
I agree one should try
before God declares it dry.

I have dreamed of you again tonight.
It was a confused sequence
of word and incident without an actual
happening, a film jumbled in
someone else's time, one in which
people can be many other things,
according to place, at the same time.
Someone said you had been sent
away to the remotest jail in the land,
and there was the evidence:
a harsh-cut wall for rooms made of rock
and a guard with the rifle and dour face.
Then someone said you had been
made a Captain and were in good hands –
your own: and I saw faces I had seen,
or not seen at all, equally, and was
convinced. You see in this my nightly calling
how illogical things are, just like
but no better planned than our lives?
You are captive and your own prison;
you are lost to us, yet not.
Carrion-crows and the State's soldiery
can not feed long on the human flesh,
and, thanks to hope, there isn't exactly
the vulture and the mouse afield,
nor are you the bird of prey;
yet who will trust a dream?

How you stood for the last picture
in the album, siding with the ironical
bougainvillaea of a murky beach in Karachi,
and promised not to meddle with
such things.
This dream is going on and denies
your whereabouts, if and how you are.
I am not certain about its ending.

I am in the farms
within ten minutes of leaving
my place. Cowbells summon
the seeker of sounds
before he can choose a path
he thinks he can trek
without spraining an ankle.
I do not wear red socks,
fearing idiomatic bulls
– who could take it out
on a rag, yet my toes
itch for the dust
of these creatures   indolent
in the lime-scented miles
round about. I often squeeze
them into an eyeball and follow
the half-moons on the grounds
postmarked. The signs cease
much too soon,
much in the manner of signs.
For a moment I think
I am lost, and as I rebuke
my sense of direction, and the
woolly barriers of hills,
from somewhere the tintinnabulations
once again
begin.

Neither this Time / Nor that Place (1984)

PRAYER

The dust-storm rose
from each corner
this past Thursday,
holy time for my ancestors
who used to pray

with such excuses
each letter of the calendar
and figures
               geometrical, sacred,
or round.

Dust-bound, like a prayer
that keeps no time in this place,
I cursed the Great Grinder
who grinds
               such fine dust it blinds everyone.

And each time in my face He blew
his dirty rejoinder.

1

Doubt enters the liveable town
like a dust-storm;
its people grey to the bone,
its objects a Babylonian nondescript.
We shake them,
hold   the film against our breath
and recover   a paperweight
(whose earlier state must
in the glacial past have been
                    the igloo),
the pencil-sharpener which was a gift,
                    a bright orange.
A friend comes in
a white shirt.
He would like to sing.

2

Friday picnic at the river
still reverberates
with the bells
announcing fish.
The reeds in the water hold the line,
hold the bells, and let go
the clever fish.

The fisherman, bundled up in a khes,
is talking to the boy
who has endless questions
about boys and fish.
We walk by on the silver sands of the Chenab,
peeling tangerines.

3

Soon the day passed into a dream.
The boat, having described a wide circle,
grounded gently
on the gravel of the river-bank.
The boatman went off
to his lodgings in town. The fisherman
and his boy packed the two fishes
they had caught and wound back the line.
A cycle-rickshaw waited for us.
With the sun setting behind her,
my wife motioned it nearer.
          We got in and it took off.
                                        Although

          it is not a chariot
drawn by seven horses with wings,
the cycle-rickshaw moves fast.
Nothing melts, no one falls out
or gets hurt.
                    It can patch up
                    time past
                    with any other time,
with just one complete motion of the wheel.

4

This is the place,
neighbour to a grand confluence
of Punjab's five rivers,
                    where all time's tortuous,
                    muddy, opaque streams
                              lose their names for once
and clarify:

here a new language
could have been born.
                    Has time begun to silt?
I open a shelf.
                    A kind of sand flies
from the ancient manuscripts.
I hope to understand
                    but for a thousand years or more
                    Arabic has held the secret
                    in an open palm.
It may be oblivion,
but I forget the word.

                                    Later,
later, I find myself in a Wild Life Park.
It is billed as a jeepable Purgatory.
A sandy plain with trees
                    and a reflecting canal through it;
                    and four black bucks from Denmark.
                    A jolly Major, who is himself fit
to be photographed by the National Geographic,
explains how the Park works
and what respective roles
people must have
to make it work.
A plucked porcupine's quill is offered me
on the spot. He thinks I am a writer
and may have use for it.
                    I know it is original
                    and will fetch a price somewhere,
                    or will not.
The porcupine, captive,
                    shrieks.
                    The sand is too hot for my poems;
                    I am sorry.

5

An elephant passes
by the Bachelor Faculty's Bungalow
every evening,
swinging its trunk through the long
summer afternoon now shrunk
                    to the size
of a toothpaste tube.

                    Brushing my jacket
            I hear the suggestion:
How about visiting your classes
on this elephant tomorrow?
It's three miles,   and my first appearance.
The elephant carries on
with his duties,

                    running fodder to the stables,
                free rides for children,
                and a sense of amazement.

6

Indoors, all winter long, tea
is served day and night.
There are poems to keep you company,
                    and friends who care.
Heavens, heavens! I say.
The evenings are a shade blue.   Yellow flowers
fill the patchy lack of green.
You often spot a black heifer in the bright
cottonfields, a soldier appears in
battle-black, a child cries.

The tamarinds guard the walks
                    and seem to listen,
their fruit dangling
like African earrings.
                    I shake one by its trunk,
but hardly a sparrow flies
out of it.

   7

The lorries from Karachi
growl on the bridge overhead.
The river at winterend is so thin,
only the sharpest pencil
will draw it on a map. Without a doubt,
the desert, this Cholistan of more than a thousand years,
                    spreads across.
Here I am planted like a silence.
There is nothing else that I can point to,
not even a tree-stump in a mile   can field the hope
that here one day   something beneficent will grow.

Inland and Other Poems (1988)

1

Here's that bush
which has all Lahore aglitter
with acacias. In March, time
begins to find small decorations
for itself, seasoning its winterhabits
to a new mildness.
The diagonal light comes down kindly,
filtering as if through leaves
which the spring has yet to hang
on our northern trees –
the floral cotton of curtains
in an urban livingroom.
There is a flutter in the slightest
suggestion of a breeze.
Each sun-dappled street of the city
confabulates a picture
at the other end of a long look.
The guesswork future of its formal gardens
only God knows –.
But for now the sunlight climbs
along the trellis (its silverskin
surface returning the gaze) and acacias
bloom where the thought is.

2

But no photograph will suffice
for the thing.
Its metal frame is the measure
of the beginning of flowers
and their predisposed end,
with what's in-between missing.
O City, am I to look at you
through a lattice-window
and stand here in witness
of everything you do
to drag in desire?
It's got to be said.
Love is a technical win
and hardly a botanical brushstroke
of it causes suasion of the canvas.
Cameras click on staccato
and lick their night-lips
before sunrise, i.e., before
garbage-collection.
As now the monotonous patter
of words here,
as herenow that of rain against this
Wednesday's newsprint and windowpane.

They did not care when he
first spoke about it.
They had seen the famines,
wars, and migrations through,
lived off leaves of a big tree
with roots down the Mediterranean,
and on palmy days
worked it out
with the reigning gods
more or less amicably.
There was that sub-clause
about periodic tributes
or an indulgence like sacrifice;
what with it!

But there he was, telling them
something, to wit,
in the name of Allah;
in fact the One
and the Only Allah.
They wondered at the singularity,
the one complete wholeness of his thought
– one from which any part could get purchase.
They had seen the gods, in public,
and through their private keyholes;
heard them thunder or sulk;
seen them fight and compromise,
sign a treaty of peace
and go back on it,
promise fair trade

and cheat.
What did he mean
to teach them:
of a world beyond the world,
better than itself,
where everything was right?

Come off it, they said:
you sound inspired;
go write a book of poems; or see a doctor.

Whatever might keep them from it,
he said, he would continue
to hand them messages
with meanings deeper than they knew
and bring them closer
to what they did not understand:
God.   "Even if
                you brought over
the sun to shine in my right hand;
                even if
                you brought over
the moon to shine in my left hand."

I don't know what they thought;
but I love the words
and the man who spoke out
in spite of them
whatever it is he had got.

Dark times are still aglow
with light from Faiz;
all year his good words
made possible
the keeping of hours,
keeping of words, the deeds,
words. And more –
for he was the man who taught
the Muse new manners,
a meaning of grace, and filled
Urdu's mid-century rift
with ore.

1

I think they are violet, green, white
butterflies which flutter across
the reedwork trellis in the garden.
Someone says Sweet Peas;
they stop fluttering. Anyway,
I am closer to the flowers now.

2

That was one way of repudiating
distance. Not peas, the butterflies hover.
I could have pointed from behind
any window to the garden outside
which had the distance gathered to itself,
with things fluttering across.

3

I am standing – not like the hours
back there – where the house garden
is proposed.   The earth
is moist with rain and a readiness.
Names not named, but the flowers will flower.
New grass is to grow under my feet.

So what if I live in a house made by idiots?
In the last one, holes were filled with toothpaste;
was so airtight breathing became a task.
Its bomb-shelters were excellent and made
you feel ready.
This has the walls wet (from the tears it causes)
and sloughs every three months.
The floors are the best thing in it, get cleaned;
for the monsoon might blow off the roof,
yet can you imagine a house without a floor?
The lawn now has a few flowers to its credit.
But the grass keeps debiting. The municipal waters
give it further lease, and the insects introduce you minute
by minute to a part of yourself.
The sun can kiss the face and the back of its neck
at the same time. I call it a place to live.

It hasn't happened here in forty years.
Fabled ships from other kingdoms
have usually sent in smokeless signals
and quietly passed by.

It is that same Star Trek gang now
armed with the laser
and the lust to find new worlds,
galaxies better or baser
than our own,
duplicating the earth's troubles elsewhere.
The last I heard of these guys
was in connection with the Romulans,
ruled as they were by some tough cookies,
whose plans had somehow overcooked.

That was a little after the nuclear-powered
Enterprise, the grand spaceship,
was to go to the Bay of Bengal, or Dhaka.
Rumour went only thus far,
but that country fast broke in two.

Fifteen years; the shining ship
is on the horizon
over the Arabian Sea.
The bulletin says 'for rest and recreation',
and I am even flattered to know
that Karachi can provide that.
I thought only stateless ships,
strayed from their course, docked here;
which, if not the convicts, ferried European
traders, missionaries and adventurers.

Mohmmad bin Qasim did not land here
a second time: no mouth-watering
warm-water ports or resort beaches in view,
nor the shrimp factories of Debel.
And there was nothing but work, work, work.

It will be customary (and true to script)
to say: "Captain, you're welcome here
anytime with your handsome crew."
To say sorry or no will be to invoke
the other customs. But surely
your consul is impolitic
in suggesting that you come to our shore
– not to refuel, or repaint with Robbialac –
but to dump your garbage, no more.

Captain, you're a busy man
with the headphone clamped all the time
when you're not in conference or reading maps;
while Lady Peach Blossom fans the versed air
and her itchy foot taps the floor: no more.
Maybe I should speak to Mr Spock,
who is rational and real cool,
and has ears long enough to hear
what he hears.

Mai Ly, it's good you make good,
make it look what it's like,
and prove me wrong after all.
You can't be unhappy.
The news says you've crossed
far more than a street –
to go to Oxford.
You are photographed
on a two-page spread, glossy, smiling,
with your new friends,
eyes a shade dark
but there as the roman dials
of the Big Ben.
Your full-length bluejeans
will forbid one to say if
your kneecaps gleam in the rare sunlight.
The treacherous South China Sea
is washed afar. There is no telling.
Those many who are not here,
have gone down to the bottom
of where that wicked water comes from,
have only darkness to contend with.
Others in the mass graves have only
unstuffed holes in the skulls
or pits for sight.
Their eyes will not resurface
to see us, greet, or judge.
Under the circumstances, we can only make
good the bet placed on us,
as sweet Thames runs softly on.

You will actually read Physics at St Hugh's
this autumn.
Your teacher is proud and fond of metonymy.
He calls you a "shining example to us all."
And your own English is perfect
enough to say: "I love chips."

This poem followed a report in Asiaweek (15 February 1985) about a refugee girl in England, aged eighteen, who was saved from a sinking fishing boat in the South China Sea by a passing British merchant ship. The girl had fled war-ravaged Saigon at the age of thirteen with her parents and was taken to England via Hong Kong. When she arrived, she did not speak a word of English but quickly learnt the language, and did so well at school that she gained a place at Oxford University.

A FOUND NOTE: ABOUT A POSSIBLE PRECURSOR

I was shopping for China tea this morning
when money changed hands
and I got a ten-rupee note. Rather crisp,
it has a handwritten note
to someone; perhaps a handy

memory-aid for the writer himself
– not to speak of the pieties
printed by the State Bank.
It's an Urdu verse
signed Nasir, and it says:

The veil is drawn for the sensible.
Come on without a veil; I am in the glass.
Her face may be a shining mirror,
it's the drinking glass he means.
The message is out of the bottle.
I read it again and forget the tea.

I write because I must
acknowledge what I owe the fellow
who gave this matter currency.
Certainly, he did not vote,
he did not remember that he wrote
the lines, and he could not quote

Shakespeare.
This fellow used money
as scrap paper for his words.
He did not care for his note;
and before he could regale on or repent,
it's obvious he was bored, or spent.

No sound
                              but
                    birds
darting from tree
to tree.

                         Not the season
that I can think of
in any loving connection.
Too much lightness
                    of the air,

                    too many figures
                    of loss.
Spring flowers swing and fall
to the graves naturally.
                    I am reading your name.

INLAND

1

West Aliquippa, Pennsylvania,
is said to be
the only inland town in the U Ess
that can be entered or left
in just one direction.
So that going in

and out of is all one thing,
a quality of feeling;
with the scenery first going
backwards, then forwards.

2

I was born in a place so
far inland of Asia
that only the mountains,
of Himalayan attitude,
could reach up
to the open air.
Then, so high, one
couldn't have breathed.

The gay sea breezes
only crashed down
there. The new geographers
call this Vale of Tears
a monsoon.
Urdu, optimist's algebra,
dubs it Moon Soon,
as if it were only
a matter of time.

3

Now I live in a country
where each town is inland
the moment you are out of town;
the sea having shied away
more than a glacier's age ago
and granted a conical tundra
of obese rocks
rising above ancient railway
stations.

Take Zurich, with its Sackbahnhof
swallowing trains by the minute
without a burp.
Then, the Moby Dick disgorges.
The flying eels
are frisky, with the thousands
in the body of steel.

4

Take this, my train. It leaves reverentially,
on back feet,
twitching
on each hairpin bend
to bite its own tail.
Inside, they smoke.
I suffocate.
At the fifth kilometer,
a blue neon
says A I R G A T E.
I can breathe now; wish
to leave by the other side
while the current lasts.

5

Yes, I can leave this train
for that shunting there: ausserorts,
agora, Ausland.
One of these two, painted green,
will arrive. I can still
board it at any junction.
After all, it is not the train
of thought.

1

My mother writes
the farmers need the rain
for the over-dry wheat,
but implores God
to delay it at least for a week.

The daughter's to be sent
off properly; rain will
spoil things.
God listens to her sometimes.
And this was a good week.

2

Was it for Thursday?
Henna caked on the hands
of the bride-to-be.
Washed, a floral writing
kissed the hands of one

the words so pleased –
with messages
no one had ever received.
The tap on the dholak
joyfully said, O look

3

there's a bride there.
But that's my sister!
She soaked her red wedding-
dress with tears,
leaving her father's home

for one of her own
(and her husband's).
It was a mild January
day in Lahore, and couldn't have
been any better in Paradise.

4

I, lonesome here even today,
read letter after letter,
strolling the shuttered lane;
imagine the colourful hour
that must stay

in memory.
It is a fine, fine day.
The sun still shines
on a part of me.
Peach trees filter the light.

5

The hasty local downpour
cancels the vision
        in a minute.
Two men pass by.
        They shake hands.

One drops a leather glove,
        and each Razumov
        mutters something
polite.   Behind the house, unreal
wheat stalks sag to the wet side.

        In the hills
        and the fields
        under western sky
the words and the rain
        falling, falling.

WHY BLAME THE BULBUL?

Why blame the bulbul?
Rather the sound of the land itself,
a nightjar on a rusty string
or a trainwhistle going far
in the night, the steam off.

Strange that there's only a road
by the woodland house,
and the infrequent packed car
intrudes in here not
by a horn but headlights.

A crescent moon hangs over the drapes
of light music – from my side of the bed.
As my hands exchange the silken sheet
for you, I know what it is to be distracted.

ISLAMABAD 1988

1

The first spring rain
turns the smoky hills sage-green –

though not in any German sense.
Language is irrelevant, anyway,

for it is the cawing of the
supervisory crows that matters;

who fly from treetop to treetop,
partying all afternoon.

All the while, until late,
these cuddly hills move closer.

If anything is still await,
it must be the musk rose cutting.

2

I am only a city
where people work and sleep –

unlike some who lived here before,
dying or flying off like bluejays.

Where one may end up is something else;
but what one began with

and has had to leave is clear.
I am practising the saffron smile

these days; field days
if you look at my lovely sisters,

Vienna, Helsinki, Canberra.
I am really not so unnatural;

can see the point in having
a pair of fussy big brothers.

Even as I know that I am not
Phoenix – out of Arizona,

I have risen from the ashes,
and must fall in love again.

Sun and Moon and Other Poems (1992)

AUNT SALMA,

who
            embroidered   stars
          in the deep blue
shawls   with gold
or silver thread
for my mother, my wife,
and herself, now so cold.

Who can say what is enough,
will make one a life
that is true
to itself, and fairly said?
She had lost a son,
raised a daughter and sewn
missing buttons on her husband's shirt

through moist glasses, during the loadshedding.
With a sense of humour, of course:
"Bespectacled women make prime
ministers; look how one has sewn up England".
And a thing about men
that were all good words on a prayer-mat –
and would not raise the hat

to anything, or an eyebrow
to notice what has already changed
and cannot live in words alone.
Were it upto her,
she'd have twilled
the subjunctive city with crowding avenues of champac.

How then?

Crisp winter of expected patterns in the garden,
wherein each dab of colour
is to find its own leaf and branch
into the possible. You would have liked this.
The sky slowly tinged with a certain blue,
while a good woman rules the land
to a new habit of sure light.

The stars were some help.
But you not here to speak to,
I must write.

Sirji, do you recall that
I have submitted myself
on this subject before. It is now after,
but I can submit my submission
again in your respect.
Our cottage industry is in boom:
five babies are produced per minute;
they come crying for international
brands of powder milk,
which is requiring canal water. They will
hopefully compete and complete with Brook Shield
one day in the 21st century.
Veil has really come down this time
– as the poet said, on men's wits;
the moon has the chance to shine out of sundry clouds
and enlighten the nation
during loadshedding.
The paddy is now standing foot
deep in sulphur, hot liquid exhausts
of the tanneries. While the politicians
are making flowery multilingual & maiden speeches,
we folk are busy
clapping for them, and catching
the content later on BBC,
Voice of America, AIR,
Doordarshan, or maybe
PTV, PBC, and BBG.
I must say that my middle-young bevy
is pulling out a special antenna to watch national tv.
I used to burn the midnight's oil before.
No charm in working any more.
Everybody here is eating money
half the week, and making the books
on the other days, looking over shoulder,

pleasing the boss but cheating Allah.
In any case, deficit is not a problem
because, INTER ALIA, SUE MOTO, and SUB JUDITH,
we can always show expense as saving
from German, Swiss, and U.S. AIDS, respectively,
verily at some physical and emotional cost to us.
Every Friday, I am praying a prayer
after namaz at durbar of Data Sahib,
two nawafil for personal help with balance sheet.
May Allah show us the right path with his own Flashlight
and ever pull us out of the straight and narrow
by a wide margin.

OFF THE WALL

(Another Found Poem in Pakistani English)

Mayor Sialkot has asked the people
to desist from writing on walls.
He said that it was against all norms
of decency to spoil the beauty
of buildings, places of worship;
was sacrilege and profanation
of the sanctity of mosques, temples,
and gurdawaras to use them
for personal advertisement.
(Of course worshipping in public
is no personal advertisement.)
In this case all defaulters shall be
legally proceeded against in future.
For the present this same writing
appears on that same wall –
but only as a bad thing for a good purpose,
washable in the rain coming from Jammu –
this ink made in Japan, and quite small.

I can hardly hear what is said.
Your words are a blizzard
in the Alpine wasteland
I have here come across.
I am all alone, without a manual,
the hiker's hype, or his tent.
I was going somewhere else;
led up the garden path;
travelling light, with more
love in my rucksack
than sausages.
No one to call, from here;
nothing to reach out to,
except the chilled echo of a thought
I am sure was you.

It has passed,
for time is still not certain
and as well policed
as the spaces we must deal with.
Why bother with that would-be
garden spring already soiled
with Neanderthaler biochemical slick?
What can the sluggish inland
waters connect?
There are no seas to surge forward;
no kindly winds in which the cyclamen blows.
The sky has no stars;
it's a wintry flammable blue
borrowed for a day.
And that blasted apple-bough
has the computer's memory, but docs not talk.

SUN AND MOON

(For Aniq – when old enough to read it)

1

Sunday was the best day
to play ducks and drakes
with one's spare time at riverside,
not so pink-hedged by the weeklong thrift,
the water almost level with the land
and often kissing the lower bank mushroom
of every ten days ago
and its side gravel.

The resident brown snail there,
every Sunday, was seen airing slowly
his awkward opinions;
the tv antennae on his twopin head transmit
the double-entendre
of the habitual wet's grouting
in the country's passhole.

One could also have one's lone sausage
with potato salad, or go Fanti
with one's girl and the self-made fire
from dry pine sticks.
Almost a perfect day,
instead of counting the blackshirts
that still lurk in the Alpine woods.

Could I then change places,
see that I may be becoming part of that
which is not part of me?
The trees around me dropped their leaves,
shook off their birds, and made
the autumn-beds of their brown leaves
often enough to make more autumn songs.
But I the same always; always the same;

too much the same.
The woman I loved was made of meerschaum
and one Swiss monsoon broke in two.
Love moved out; the tree-barks darkened in the face;
the river froze over;
the land sighed beneath the early snow
of its absences.
The world – its affairs, arias of intent,
offices – ganged up on me.

2

Sibelius, your seemingly silent bust in that other wood
is one with the snow and its wintry mind;
and in time is green, fernlike again
in the notes made of your country's air.
Yes, it is possible, elsewhere,
that an orchestral intention is realized
in being read so well by nature.
I am not promised any such nor have recourse
to what's in the ear but will not ring out
in the time that remains.
Yet, strangely, as I write this,
tears come down like a rain that strings all instruments,
making new channels of grief in this poem
and across that continent of pain.

3

Is sadness a formation of land
across all waters,
in which the inland seas of joy and grief
mutate like Moving Rocks
to wash on an invisible shore?

Sadness is the only constant sun
melting one away;
each minute one gives up a bit more,
until the sun sets upon its own consequence.

How am I to change the laws of motion,
replace the continents into those symmetries
of love on which the moonlight
will not be a blemish;
hate not exceed love;
love's analogies not become its functions;
one's own life not stretch itself beyond one's gift?

4

Each day is a live wire
passing thought to the illogic of its conclusions:
a flame-tree's brilliant red or yellow flowers,
as if it were a sunset in the Margallas;
an image on which to fix myself
and, possibly, mint memory back into desire,
all my other coinage spent in Europe's shopping centres.

Son, when you were 3
and one day your mother said "You are my good son",
you replied "Not moon?" and laughed a knowing laugh,
as if the tangled planets and the stars over us
could hold the language for that one day
to a feeling that would stay,
meanings to remain for all just the same.
The family's language has changed in the meantime;
– you have lost your English and your Urdu,
and now you speak only German.
But you, to me, are still both: my son, my moon,
in this same sky arching

between places.
Life translates like that.
Time lapses but, somehow,
is always present to deal with.
In the house-garden here, a tall,
many-branched tree grows with fine leaves.
In the moonlight, with no one watching,
vagrants from the neighbourhood come around,
aiming their stones sometimes
to take from it what they can;
or smooching the pear-shaped fruit
ripe on its branch,
which surpasses all titular explanations
of the spring, its sovereign flower
in the sunlight gone,
transparent as Monday or Saturday,
both its timely announcements
pendulous on the stem.

For once the forecast has been correct.
I speak to her across miles of rain
(this beautiful woman I've just met)
by telephone, and tell her in the main
that I like the fine lilt of her voice,
and would phone again, were it my choice.
She agrees but cannot see through the April shower
that the old apple-tree here has its first flower.

If only the full-moon could say it fully;
it declines here mid-sentence
to illumine what you said to me
in another town hundreds of miles away.
I have to put on my carlights
to see how the once-in-bloom jacarandas
row after row drop their mauve silently;
little birds in May nesting.

That is to say it's this makes me speak up
or at least write in the time of year,
in the same off-moonlight,
moving past as if into that same flower:
your body's scent this minute, this hour –

which can ease this city anytime
into an efflorescence of trees.

One must have a native tongue
in which to make love – is said
to be echt, realpolitik. Yes,
I have only English to make do.
What else will help anyway?
In Urdu, the tongue unites with language
in the same word, lying taut
in verbal saliva;
works like a wire service,
here draws the correct reply.
My love, I will brook
no distances between us –
say it so as I may
in the only truthful words that I know;
and will blow on hard and long enough
to dry up the monsoon air
so it may conduct these messages.
Even if the tongue may not touch you there,
I hope my language will.

They are waltzing their military bum into the Mediterranean
and the Gulf between us.
Sea-curdling vessels plough through here day after day.
They are converting nomadic sand-dunes into casinos
of death where mortar shells will be the roulette prize.
They are hooded, masked men into oil or grease
and they have still better things in store.
Where the Adonis fondled once the language plants
and the yellow and crimson petals grew on elongated,
globular shapes of meaning, a Babel is being built again.
From the secret sluices of the Tigris in the sandy plain
a new language struggles to be born.
Ishtar's eyelashes will be plucked
and buried in unmarked ground.
Is this the karbala? Each generation's karbala?
This desecration is not the last, nor will stop at the land's end.
What is spoiled now will improve in time,
like the local grape into champaign, your taste in the mouth;
the haj will be in English.

July to August the rains
will delay flower setting in the cotton
                        (the one place to hide this sentiment),
                streaming windowpanes
        will level with the sky,
and the flights will be cancelled so often
that I'll need to think twice about love.

No need to look for any signs above.
This land cannot support such notions.
Petrol strike, mail blockage, thought police
and censored letters, bad telephones even bugged,
prying eyes fixed in every tree,
forbidding homes with myriad little screen doors
and limping bastards in the neighbourhood
have not changed, have been the same
for a thousand years; (though
now they all have a new address and a modern name).
Don't I know this trough?
                        Every summer,
the Chenab still overflows with old malice.
Were you only to hold my hand from across,
the state would collapse. Where shall we go?
Love's always on trial here; the caravels
of escape beached in the last brown delta.
I'll wait here until you fax me, whenever
it's possible. I may have an idea then.

CRUSOE'S ISLAND, 1976

The French gun in the park has dated.
It is aimed at the water.
Long silent, it still fires a contour shot
into the island's body, its angular map.
I read as I walk along,
these words that time has written here
wave after wave after wave
of the ancient, emerald sea.
The last one broke against the shore at midnight.

A breakfast of fresh coconut
and a solitude that might tempt a Columbus
to change his plans, take a local woman,
move into a makeshift beach hut
and try to forget with her
the secrets that the northern sea holds.
Her black hair as long as the rowing
back to Spain. Why write the journal?

Actually, he landed more than twenty
miles across, long before the mango
was indentured from India.

I step out of the clump of palm and sugarcane
to view the postcard sky in real sunlight.

No, I am glad of the water that connects fairly
and disconnects. I do not want a road
built across the sea to the far-off, rich
destinations; only the island's rippled
speech in my left ear,
the succulent texts written at their own pitch.

Tobago / Zurich
October, 1983

I xerox my kisses and post them
          weekly before they're cold.
          She does likewise,
          hoping the envelope will arrive
          as addressed, the commerce thrive
          without the censor and the local scold
          catching this loop or that leery hem
          still warm, life-like.

Public, we wear
love as lightly as possible
and celebrate the laissez-faire
when we're not short either
of passage or postage.
If we travel any wider,
we are shortchanged;
stay indoors for safety,
making the unseen flowers grow.

I say my passion for you will move the earth
– the dates nearer the desire.
          (You have heard that one before?
          Do lovers still replay old tapes for you?)
Your silent look stops the earth in its course.

I say my heart will break so.
          Next day's papers write death across the page.
          It's put to 6.8 on Mr Richter's scale –
          and declared, all in all,
          the epicentre was Upper Chitral.

1

Cordoban,
step into a new pair of shoes.
There, your footprints in the azure
stretching over Andalusia!
Go softly through its lanes.
The city melts in the mouth
like candy floss.
What remains is relict.

2

The Guadalquiver divides here less
from the force of water – the riparian
rites of the Berbers not forgotten –
than the leathersmell flowing
from one end to the beginning;
man-smell, skin-smell;
the smell of conquest and vanquishing;
the almond blossoms on trees nodding
to the south wind.

3

History abuts here again
to its own explanations;
the Alcázar's Roman bridge,
the river meandering across
the fields of cotton, corn, and barley
to the Atlantic Ocean;
new electrical fittings, of course,
and chapters of endless olives.

4

Outside the lichened Arabic walls
Averrös waits,
while the city's angels take new language courses
and operate the official grapevine.
But you haven't walked out of it yet –
a white handkerchief across the city's face.

5

Near La Masqita
and let heaven's music fill in for light –
turn the shadows in the nave
back to the rows, people.
So you will not avert
the breezes from the Yemen
or your silent prayer
through this watchful arch of time
(to a God who will bless
without design, not convert).

WINTER FLIGHT

(For Farid-ud-Din Attar – with apologies for lateness)

From Western Siberia to Pakistan,
6000 kilometres, they fly:
the bustard, sand grouse, crane, wader.
All to choose their own salt ranges.

The cranes are wintering in Baluchistan.
Waders, of course, take a separate route,
dispersing to the smell of wind and water,
from orchards hung down from heaven, warm.

And there is other waterfowl, diffuse,
but with a cultured sense of direction:
ducks, geese, egrets, herons, storks,
flamingos, spoonbills, ibises, coots;

even ospreys, falcons, eagles.
Nothing wishes to be left behind.
Starlings, too, are homely watercolours
in our lawns, partying

mornings on fruit and berries;
or insects in the afternoon. Such a place to be!
Plant by plant, the gardens are lined
with grasshopper, locust,

caterpillar, cutworm, and beetle.
They will feed on them in conference
and breed in the summer, without talk.
As per report this month,

one lakh Afghans and Pakistanis also
will stay back in Russia,
wed Soviet women, instantly
take to borsch and balalaika

and sing the year more cordage
for an anchor. Happy birds,
sail in the wind, sail on the sea.
Your names and feathers are a joy to me.

POST SCROTUM

(In Memoriam Samuel Beckett)

Watt? Yes. But the same when the Mal'oun died
in the island; this island severed,
repoussé, reeling with peat-reek;
this drizzle of grief –
interminable falling on the wide sea.
Moll's face saffron-coloured, hair like
petals plucked from a white chrysanthemum;
local boys on stout or busy at hurling;
and our scriveners, on regular beat up in London,
aping accents of the English gentry.
I broadcast in Irish then, from Radio Éireann,
the right embers and all that fall to the ashes
or whatever I often whispered to myself
through Murphy, Philips, or Grundig.
No, not Grundig, for the word grounds the air,
the mind slips out of form in that language,
is not hand in glove as now. Example:
with a handschuh your hands feel they wear shoes;
the foot's in the mouth; and you write with your feet.
Paris is O.K. Paris is all right. Paris is O.K. All right.
I was lecteur d'anglais in that place, teaching Doublin'
English and writing like Thom A. Becket what no one,
except J. J. in some arseholy state or other, would attempt –
in a language of my own.
I hear now that across the Chunnel
one side tells the other it's French I wrote;
the other side calls it English, or by other appelatives;
such as would divide the protestant cake in catholic portions
and make for a nice debate
in the Parliament of European Foules.
If I said Parnell was no string-pulling
politician, women would be tightening the girth

of their drawers with double-knotted strings.
I left because truelove had run out of the vein,
the earth turning no end but negative;
its slow poisons free a sweet violet in my lungs.
And, yes, French had a point or two.
That dusty potato dropped in 1921 or 1845,
it named the apple of the earth –
to say nothing of the rotten core.
Peeling. Peeling.

Alamgir Hashmi has been writing poetry for the last forty years. He won the poetry prize in the All-Pakistan Creative Writing Contest in 1972 and the Patras Bokhari Award (National Literature Prize) of the Pakistan Academy of Letters in 1985, and was the first English-language writer to bring such recognition to English writing in Pakistan. He is also widely published abroad – in the United Kingdom, Australia, India, Canada, New Zealand and the United States.

Equally well-known as author of several scholarly books, he has been Professor of English and Comparative Literature in Pakistan, Europe and the United States. He was a judge of the Commonwealth Writers Prize 1990, and a member of the 1996 jury for the Neustadt International Prize for Literature.

John Kinsella is a prolific writer and author of over 25 books, and has published poems in literary journals internationally and has received a number of literary awards, including a Young Australian Creative Fellowship and a two-year Fellowship from the Literature Fund of the Australia Council.

In 1998, he took up residence in the UK, where he is Fellow of Churchill College, Cambridge University. He is also Adjunct Professor to Edith Cowan University, Western Australia and Professor of English at Kenyon College in the United States.

Since 1998, he has been International Editor for Arc Publications, with whom he has published two collections, the first of which – The Undertow: New and Selected Poems (Arc, 1996) – was his first UK edition. A third collection, Lightning Tree, is being brought out by Arc in 2003.

Also available in the
ARC PUBLICATIONS
International Poets series

LOUIS ARMAND (Australia)
Inexorable Weather

ROSE AUSLÄNDER (Germany)
Mother Tongue
TRANSLATED FROM THE GERMAN
BY JEAN BOASE-BEIER AND ANTHONY VIVIS

DON COLES (Canada)
Someone has Stayed in Stockholm

SARAH DAY (Australia)
New & Selected Poems

GAIL DENDY (South Africa)
Painting the Bamboo Tree

KATHERINE GALLAGHER (Australia)
Tigers on the Silk Road

ROBERT GRAY (Australia)
Lineations

MICHAEL S. HARPER (U.S.A)
Selected Poems

DENNIS HASKELL (Australia)
Samuel Johnson in Marrickville

DINAH HAWKEN (New Zealand)
Small Stories of Devotion

RICHARD HOWARD (U.S.A.)
Trappings

ANDREW JOHNSTON (New Zealand)
The Open Window
JOHN KINSELLA (Australia)

The Undertow
The Silo:
A PASTORAL SYMPHONY
Lightning Tree

JOHN KINSELLA (ed)
Landbridge
AN ANTHOLOGY OF CONTEMPORARY AUSTRALIAN POETRY

EVA LIPSKA (Poland)
Pet Shops & Other Poems
PARALLEL-TEXT EDITION POLISH / ENGLISH, TRANSLATED FROM THE
POLISH BY BARBARA BOGOCZEK AND TONY HOWARD

THOMAS LUX (U.S.A.)
The Street of Clocks

J. D. McCLATCHY (U.S.A.)
Division of Spoils

MENGHAM, R., PIÓRO, T. & SZYMOR, P. (eds)
Altered State: The New Polish Poetry
PARALLEL-TEXT EDITION POLISH / ENGLISH

MARY JO SALTER (U.S.A.)
A Kiss in Space

TOMAZ SALAMUN (Slovenia)
Homage to Hat and Uncle Guido and Eliot
SELECTED POEMS
EDITED BY CHARLES SIMIC, INTRODUCTION ROBERT HASS,
TRANSLATED FROM THE SLOVENE BY
CHARLES SIMIC, ANSELM HOLLO ETC.

C. K. STEAD (New Zealand)
Straw into Gold
The Right Thing

ANDREW TAYLOR (Australia)
The Stone Threshold

JOHN TRANTER (Australia)
The Floor of Heaven

www.ingramcontent.com/pod-product-compliance
Lightning Source LLC
Chambersburg PA
CBHW032253070726
47590CB00016B/2595